tDCS Journal & Montage Placement Guide

This book is not intended as a substitute for the medical advice of physicians. The reader should regularly consult a physician in matters relating to his/her health and particularly with respect to any symptoms that may require diagnosis or medical attention.
(health, alternative healing)

The information provided in this book is designed to provide helpful information on the subjects discussed. This book is not meant to be used, nor should it be used, to diagnose or treat any medical condition. For diagnosis or treatment of any medical problem, consult your own physician. The publisher and author are not responsible for any specific health or allergy needs that may require medical supervision and are not liable for any damages or negative consequences from any treatment, action, application or preparation, to any person reading or following the information in this book. References are provided for informational purposes only and do not constitute endorsement of any websites or other sources. By using tDCS you do so at your own risk.

tDCS Journal & Montage Placement Guide

By

Tobias Zimmerhoff

Dedication

To every tDCSnaut who is navigating
their way out of the maze.

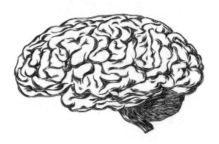

Mind over matter, but what really matters, when matter clutters the brain, filling it with chatter - Matter matters in this matrix of the mind, the labyrinth so complex, yet divine, it's easy to lose all hope as matters creep in and foresight is displaced and tomorrow seems dim. For today, the pressures of life have taken one into the pit of the gray, the darker regions of the enclave .

There is hope for the matters that blind the path, the dark maze of confusion the matters do craft; twist and turn, through narrow burrows, the stone walls seems endless, a cycle of cloudiness, The Chatter Minotaur does impose.

The bull that has you in his clutches will give way, to the flash of the lighting of Aegeus blade. For renaissance takes place, the chatter will fade, as Theseus strikes and leads us out of the winding domain of the monsters cave; dust settling past the solar ray blast, vision increasing with each step; clarity and emotions come flooding back, as we move closer to the surface. We look out the door rising up out of the earths floor, a genesis bursts forth, in silence we observed, that the doorway has no hinges, and no door, just illumination and endless possibilities untapped to explore. Three pounds of gray, once a weight of infinity, now weaving into circuits of resilient tapestry.

Determination, perspective and empathy, open up a world of boundless possibilities, a think tank of imagination, a quantum force to shape ones reality. Mind over matter, cut through all the chatter, don't ever give up, gray matter, matters. I can see - Tobias Zimmerhoff

The tDCS Journal was created out of a need, out of a place of inspiration and necessity to help track, chart, and log ones tDCS progress. I have found tDCS to be valuable in my life and thus far experienced nothing but positive results. With that said, tDCS is no panacea. I would encourage anyone who dares to venture into this frontier, do your own thorough research and journal your results.

This book is in no way telling anyone to use tDCS, it is simply a journal, that also contains well known documented montage electrode placements.

The montages listed in this book are public knowledge. You can search and verify these placements have been studied internationally by the military, academia and the medical field. Everyone is different, what works for one person, may not work for another.

Most studies on montage placement have been done on right hand dominant individuals. If you're left handed do further research before experimenting with tDCS.

This book is not medical advice. This book is not meant to be, nor should it be, used to diagnose or treat any medical condition.

Author

10-20 (EEG) PLACEMENT SYSTEM

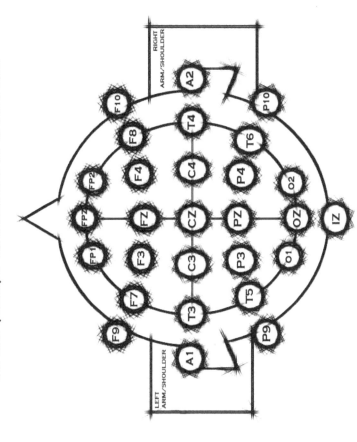

MONTAGE PLACEMENT

GUIDE

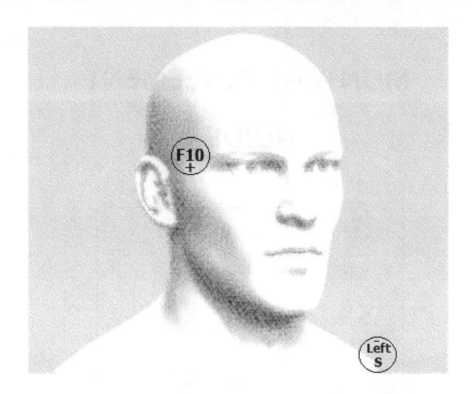

ACCELERATED LEARNING (DARPA)

STUDY EFFECT: Accelerated Learning Montage (DARPA)

This montage has been used by the military and in academic research and has been shown to increase focus and learning speed by up to 2x the average.

Anode: + Right Temple [F10]

Cathode: - Left Shoulder

Depression and Anxiety

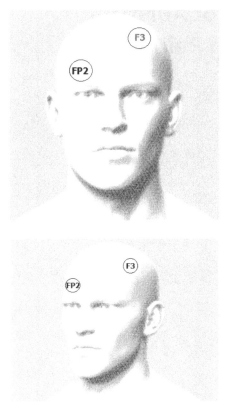

Anode: + Left DLPFC [F3]

Cathode: - Right Supraorbital [FP2]

Study Effects: Improved Mood, Reduced Depression, Reduced Anxiety

Alternative Depression Montage

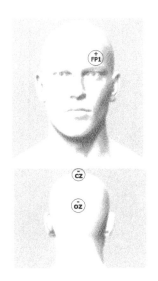

Anode: Left [FP1]

Cathode: Top of Head [CZ], Occipital [OZ]

Enhancing Motor Ability & Reducing Pain

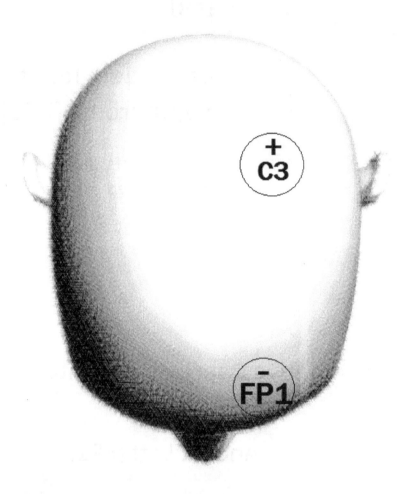

Anode: + [C3]

Cathode: - [FP1]

Motor studies have shown improvements in motor function of stroke patients, and several studies have shown reduction in pain.

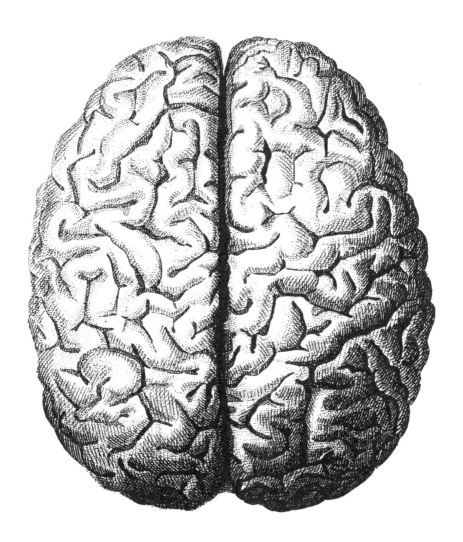

Improved Insight

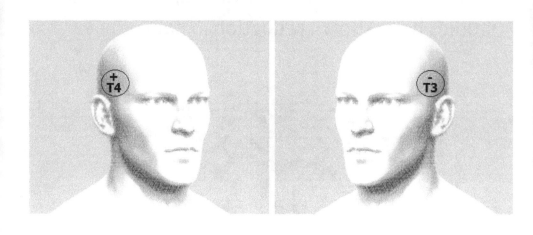

Anode: + Right Temporal [T4]

Cathode: - Left Temporal [T3]

Study Effect: Insight Improvement Problem Solving, General Cognitive Enhancement, Savant Learning

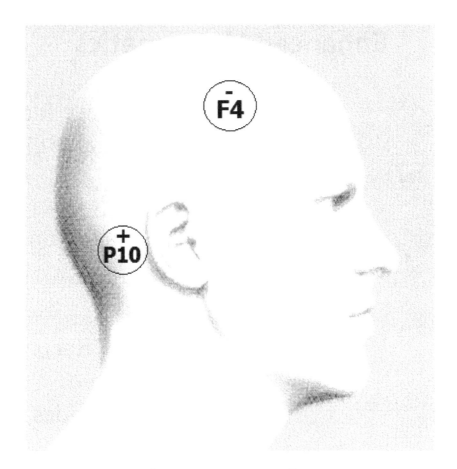

Increased Present Awareness

Anode: + Right Mastoid [P10]

Cathode: - Right DLPFC [F4]

Study Effects: Increased Present Awareness, Increased Impulsiveness , Cautious Driving

Enhanced Mathematics

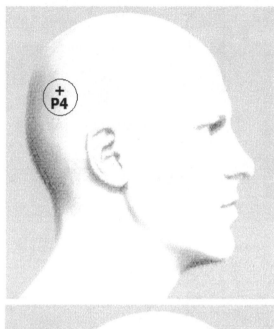

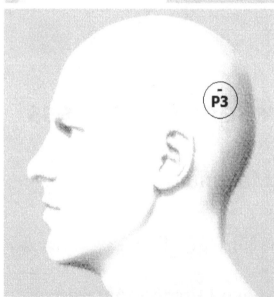

Anode: + Right Parietal [P4]

Cathode: - Left Parietal [P3]

Study Effects: Enhanced Mathematics & Numerical Abilities, Improved Understanding of Mathematics

Studies have shown that this placement can enhance mathematics learning ability for up to 5-6 months. What was most affected and retained was the material that was studied during this period.

Reduced Risk Taking

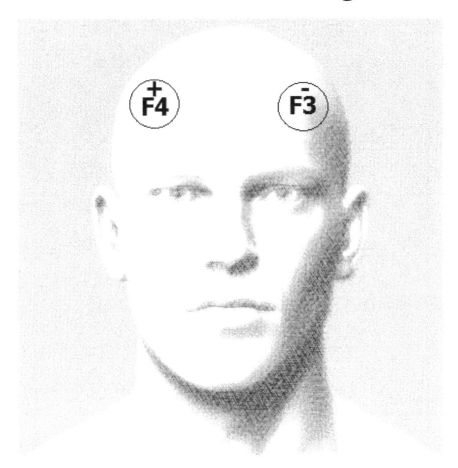

Anode: + Right DLPFC [F4]

Cathode:- Left DLPFC [F3]

Study Effects: Reduced Risk Taking, Reduced Drug & Alcohol Addiction, Impulsiveness, Reduced Appetite & Binge Eating.

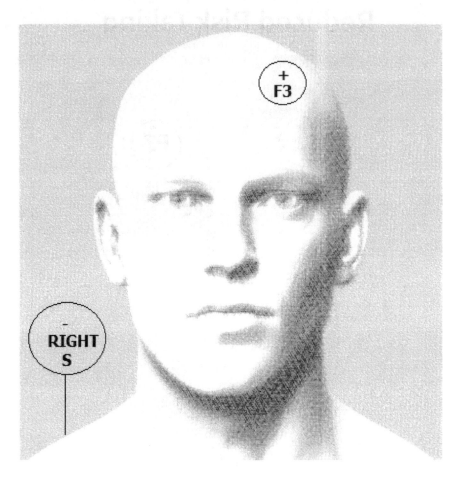

Memory and Learning

Anode: + [F3]

Cathode: - Right Shoulder

Alternative Memory and Learning

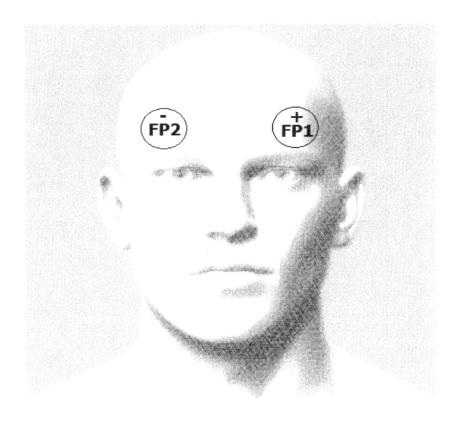

Anode: + Supraorbital [FP1]

Cathode: - Supraorbital [FP2]

Study Results: Improving Memorization & Learning

Improved Socialization

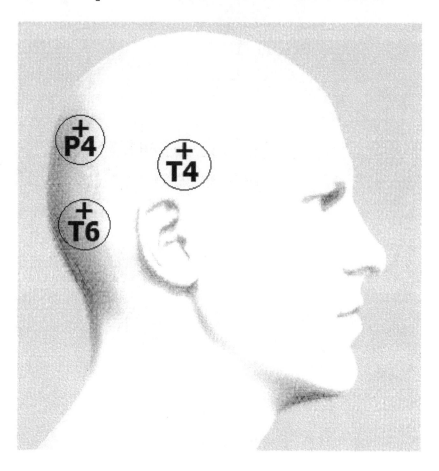

Anode: + Temporal [T4, or T6], Parietal [P4]

Cathode: - Left Shoulder

Study Effects: Improved Socialization, Social Cognition, Improved Interaction, Emotional State, Empathy

Improved Socialization

This montage has shown improvement in controlling emotional states, and emotional reactions to others. It is also known to improve and moderate empathy and motor resonance.

Anode: + Temporal [T4 or T6], Parietal [P4]

Cathode: - Opposite Shoulder

Improved Pitch Perception

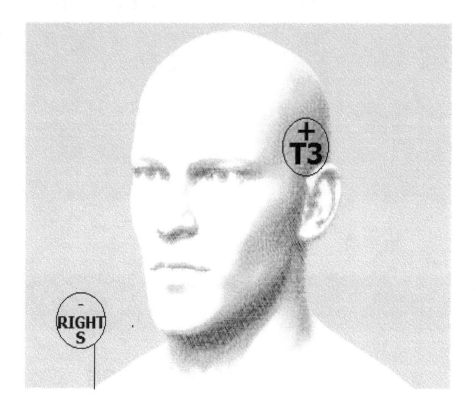

Anode: + Temporal [T3 or T4]

Cathode: - Opposite Shoulder

Study Effects: Improved General Hearing, Audio Processing,Improved Pitch Perception

Anode [+] Red	Cathode [-] Black	Target Behavior	Study
DLPFC (F3)	DLPFC (F4)	Decreased depression/ pain / increased organization	Smith & Clithero, (2009)
Central PC (FZ)	Cheek	Impulse control in ADHD	Tzu-Yu Hsu (2011)
DLPFC (F3)	Right shoulder	Decreased depression reduced food alcohol craving	Smith & Clithero, (2009)
DLPFC (F3)	Supra Orbital (Fp2)	Improved Mood	Vanderhasselt et. al., (2013)
Right Temple (F10)	Left shoulder	Accelerated Learning	Kruse (2008) DARPA
Supra Orbital (FP1 or Fp2 depending on pain side)	Neck (opposite side)	Pain reduction possible increase in impulsiveness	Mendonca (2011) Beeli (2008)
C3 and or C4	Orbital (Fp1 or Fp2)	Improved fine motor control /reduced pain opposite side of anode	Lindenberg et al., (2010), Fregni, (2006) Vineset, et. al, (2006)
Temporal (T3)	Shoulder	Improved audio processing	Ladeira, et. al., (2011)
Base of neck	Occipital (O1 & O2)	Reduced migraine pain	Antal (2011)

Anode [+] Red	Cathode [-] Black	Target Behavior	Study
Parietal (P4)	Parietal (P3)	Improved math understating / increased verbal impairment	Kadosh (2010)
Temporal (T4 & T6) Parietal (P4)	Temporal (T3)	Insight improvement / "Savant Learning"	Chi & Snider (2011)
Orbital PFC (Fp1 and/or Fp2)	Orbital PFC (Fp1 and/or Fp2)	Attention improvement	Gladwin, et al., (2012)
DLPFC(F3)	DLPFC (F4)	Reduced cigarette, alcohol, junk food craving	Fregni, et al., (2007), Boggio et al., (2007) Fregni, et al., (2007)
DLPC (F3 &F4)	Mastoid (P10 & P9)	Theta-tDCS2 Improved sleep	Marshal (2011)
Mastoid (P10)	DLPFC (F4)	Increased impulsiveness Increased present awareness	Beeli, et al., (2008), Ledoux, (1996)
Occipital (O1, Oz, and or O2)	base of neck or CZ	Improves visual motor reaction times	Anatal & Paulus (2008)
DLPFC (F4)	DLPFC (F3)	Reduce risk taking	Fecteau, et al. (2007)

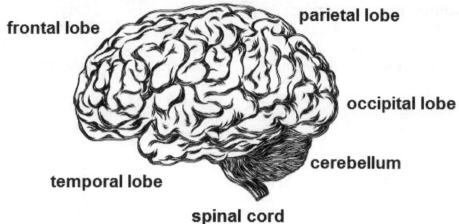

frontal lobe

parietal lobe

occipital lobe

cerebellum

temporal lobe

spinal cord

Brain Facts

* The brain contains 100 billion neurons:about 15 times more than the humans on Earth; which is about the number of stars in the Milky Way Galaxy.

*The brain has more connections than there are stars in the universe.

* The brain contains about 20 watts of power: Enough to illuminate a light bulb.

*The Brain consumes 20% of the body's energy production.

*Your brain weighs about 3 pounds. Of that, the dry weight is 60% fat, making your brain the fattiest organ.

* Humans are not getting smarter. IQ's have dropped over 13 points since the Victorian era.

* The gut is the second brain and contains 100,000 neurons. Gut bacteria make over 30 neurotransmitters, including serotonin.

*95% of decisions take part in the subconscious mind.

* The brain has no pain receptors, the brain itself can feel no pain.

*Our brains crave mental stimulation.

tDCS Journal

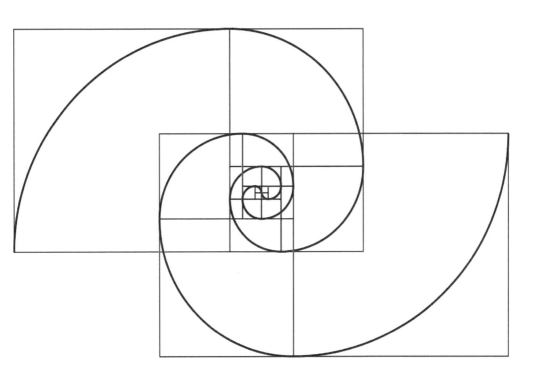

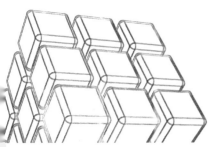

DATE

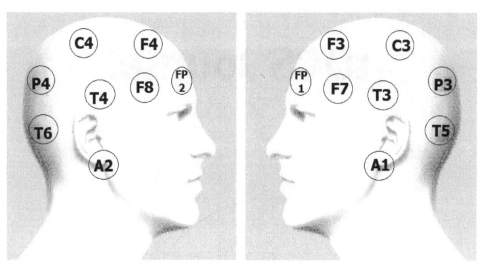

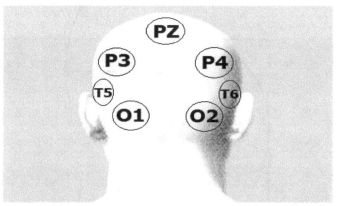

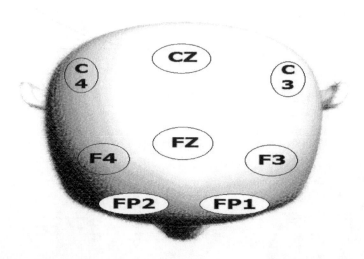

DATE

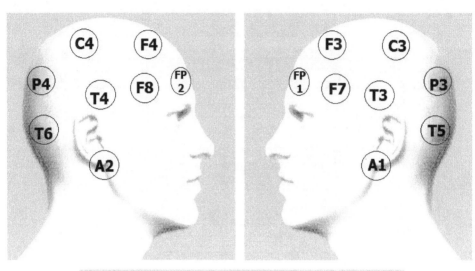

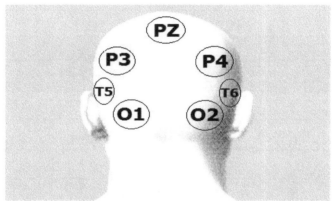

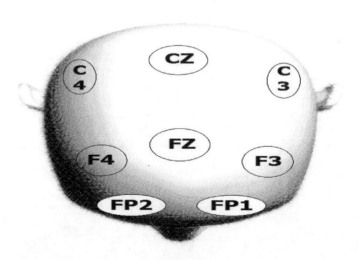

DATE

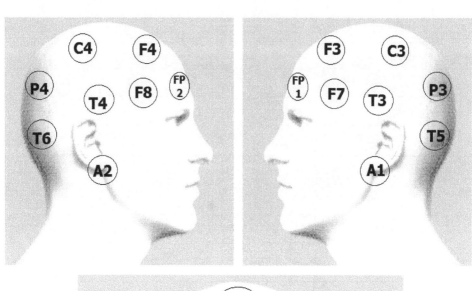

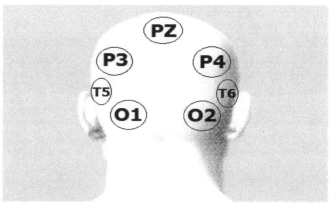

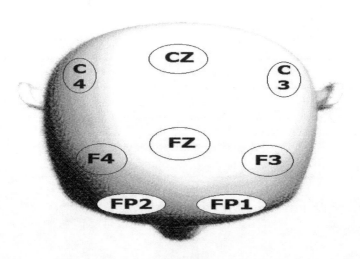

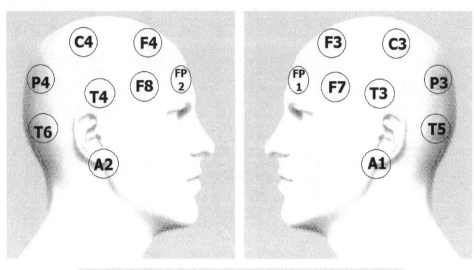

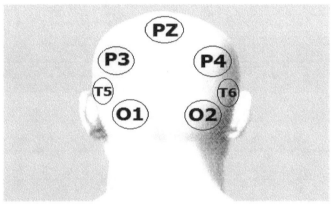

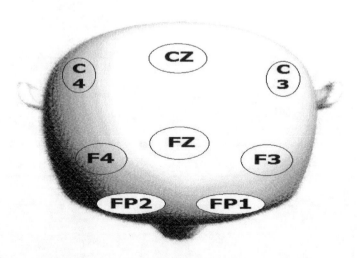

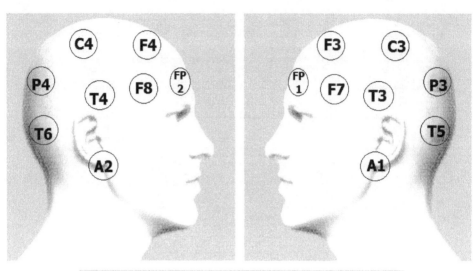

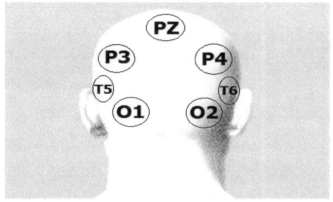

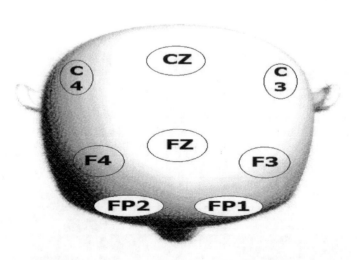

DATE

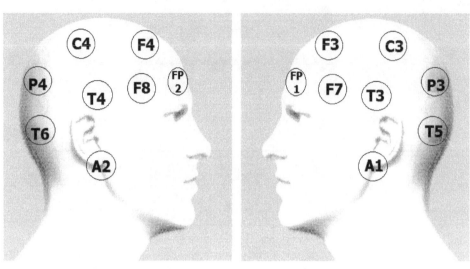

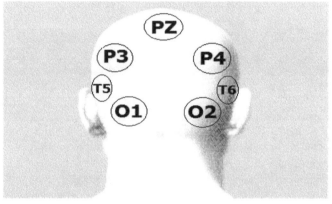

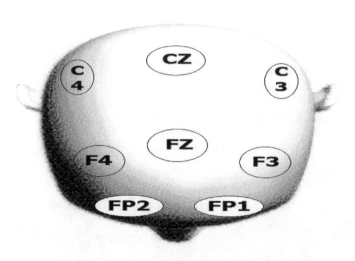

DATE

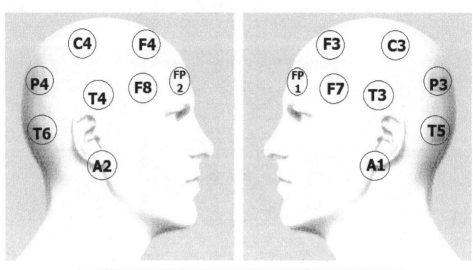

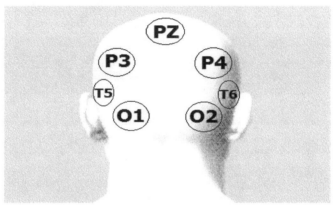

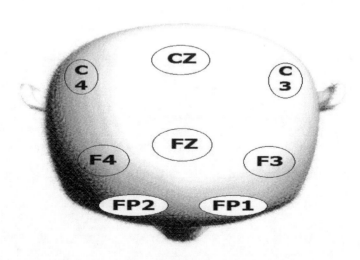

DATE

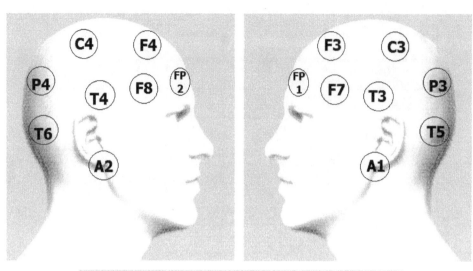

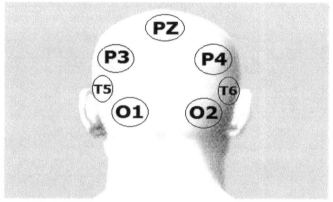

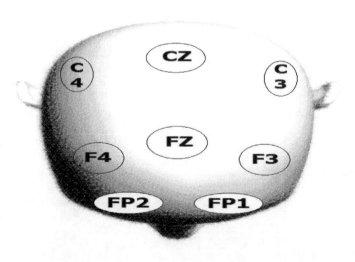

DATE

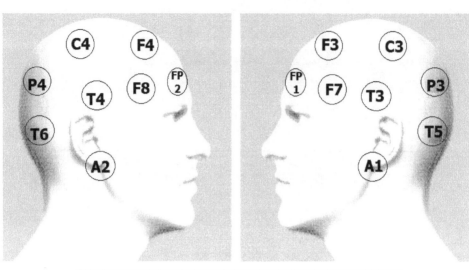

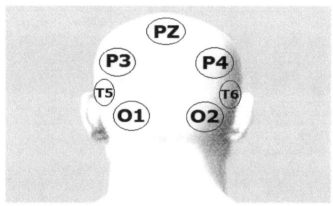

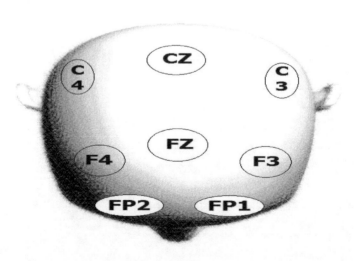

DATE

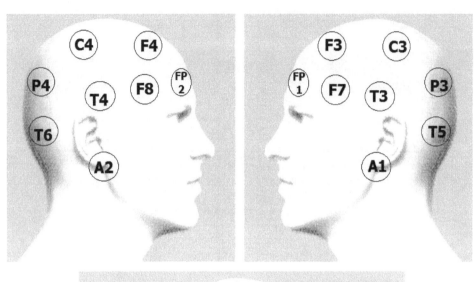

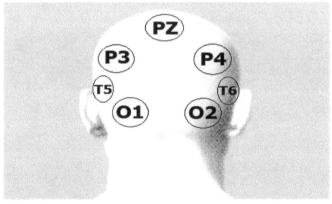

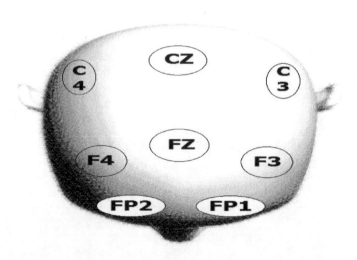

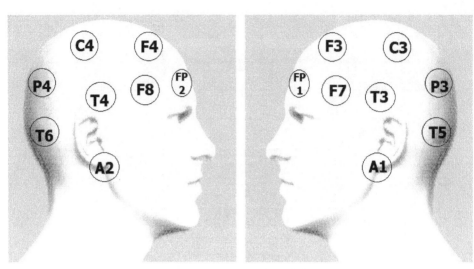

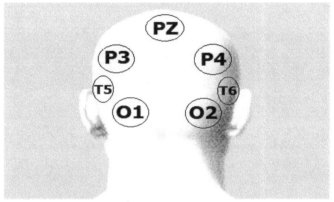

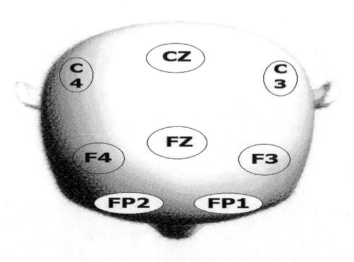

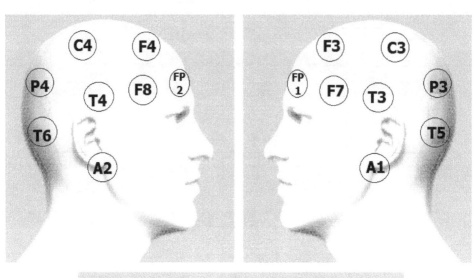

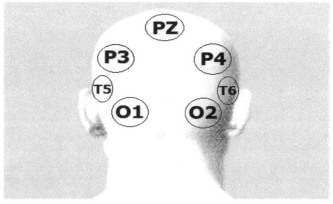

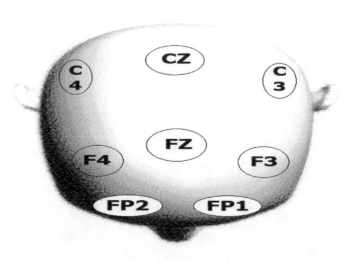

DATE

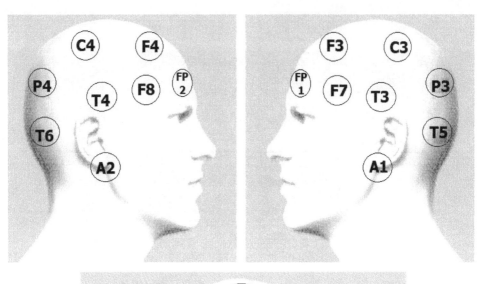

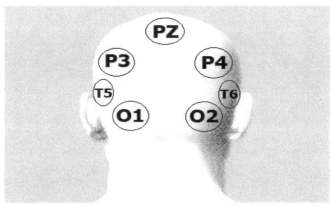

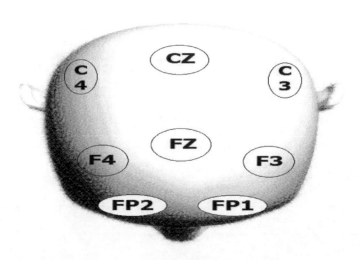

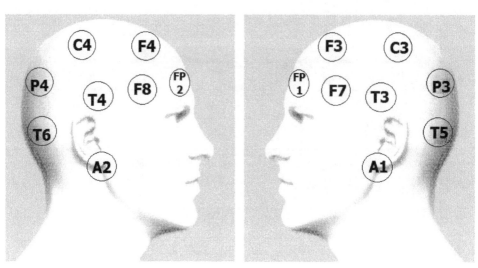

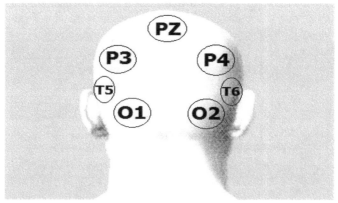

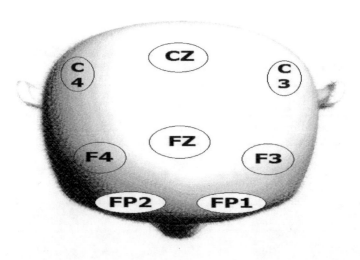

DATE

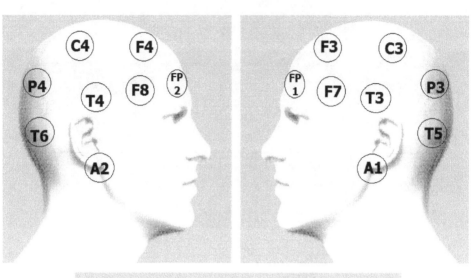

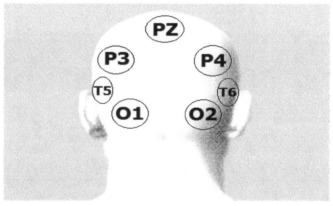

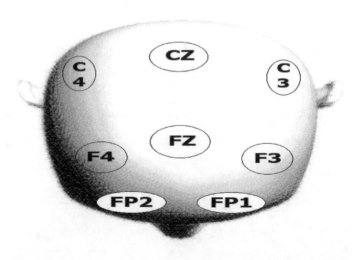

DATE

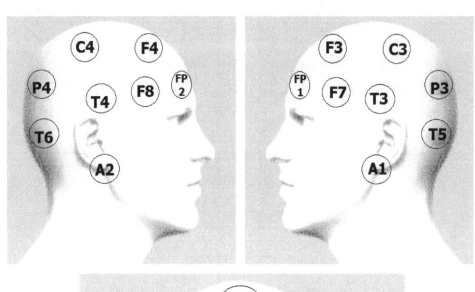

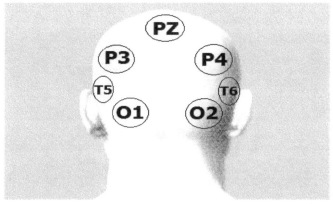

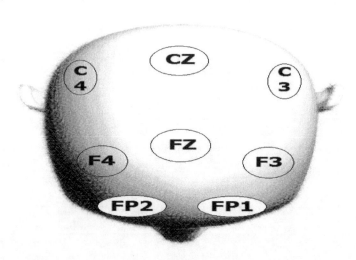

DATE

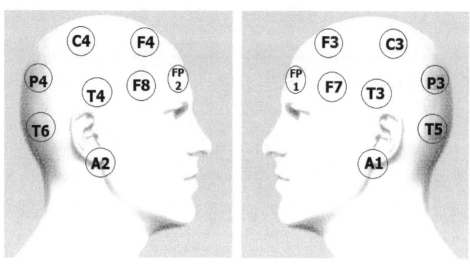

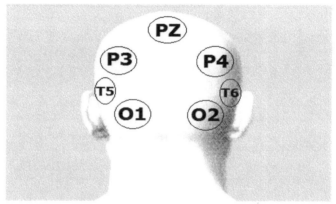

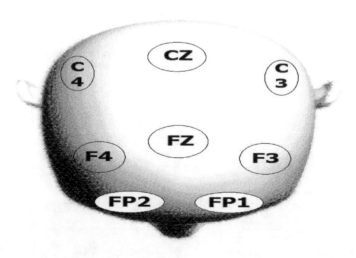

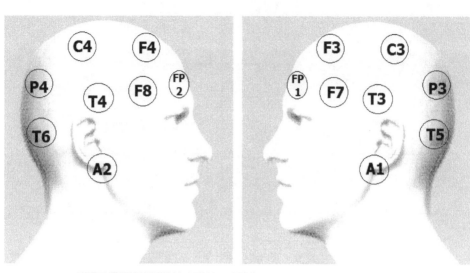

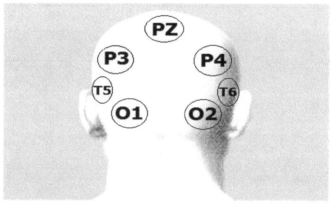

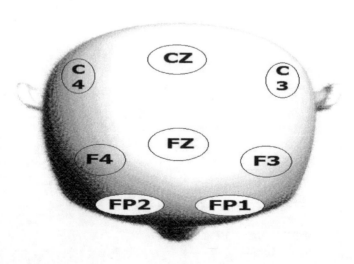

DATE

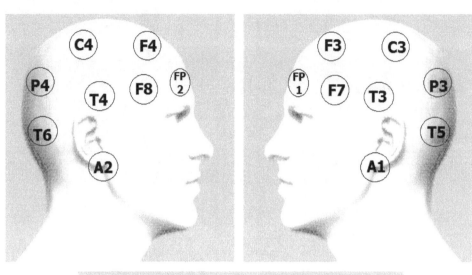

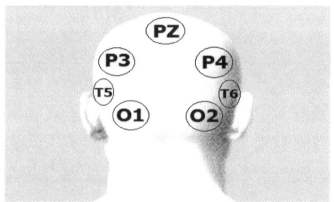

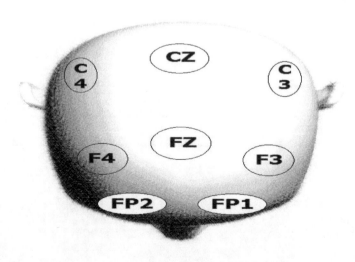

DATE

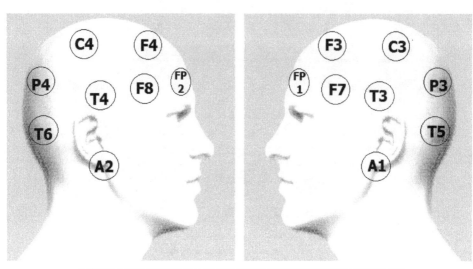

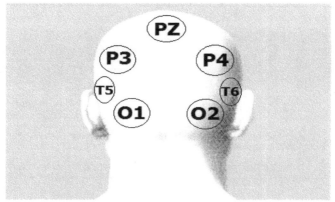

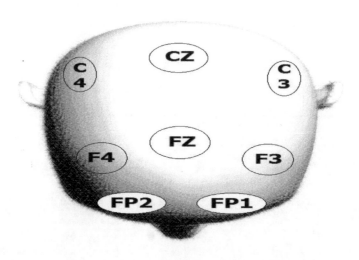

DATE

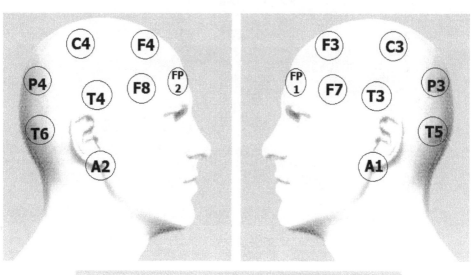

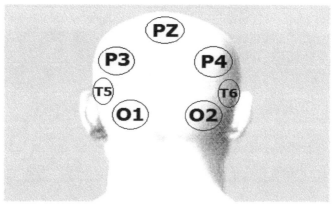

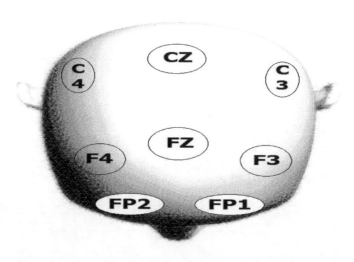

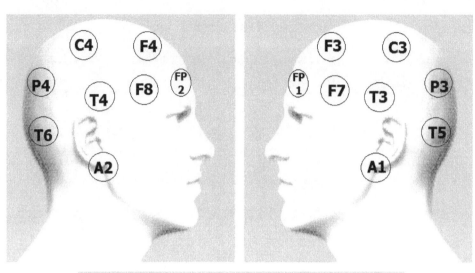

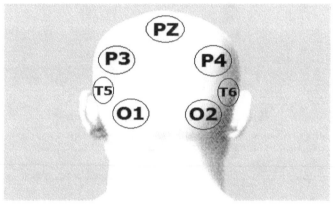

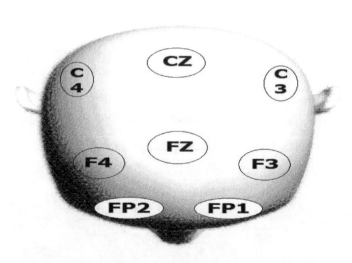

DATE

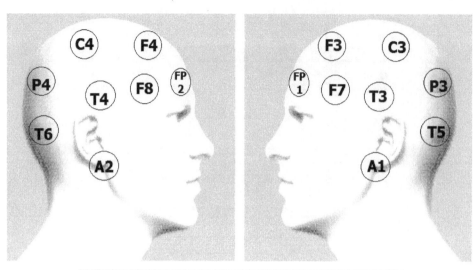

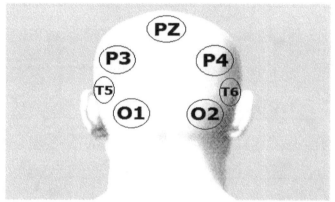

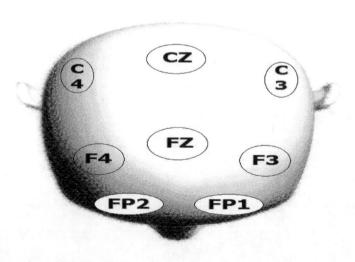

DATE

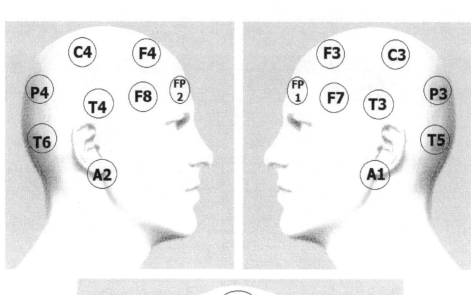

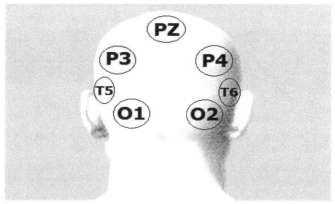

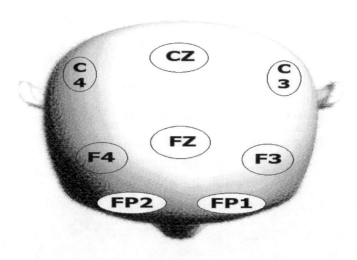

DATE

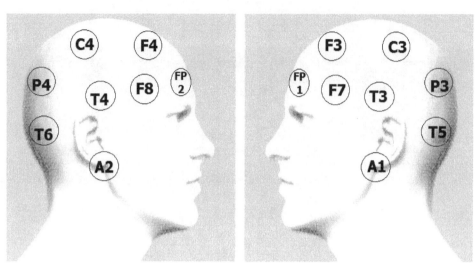

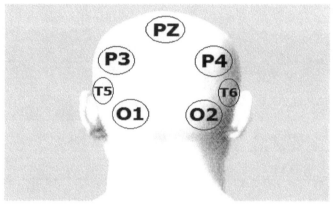

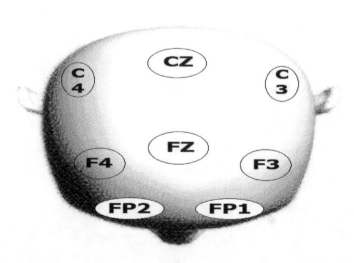

DATE

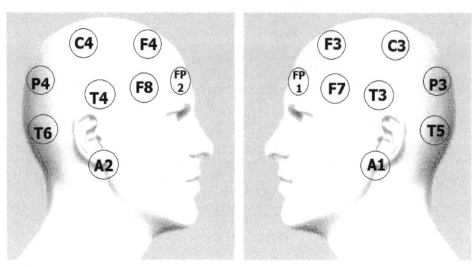

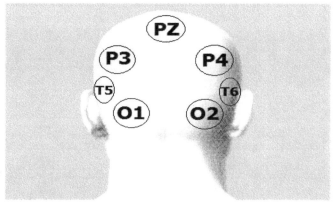

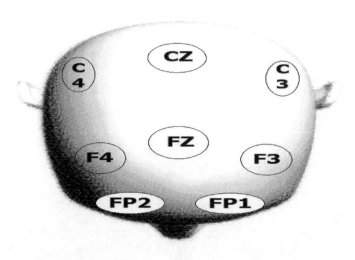

DATE

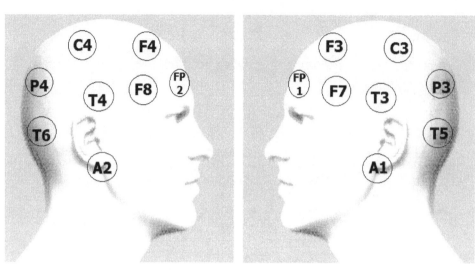

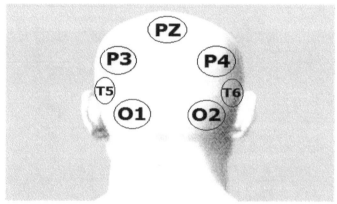

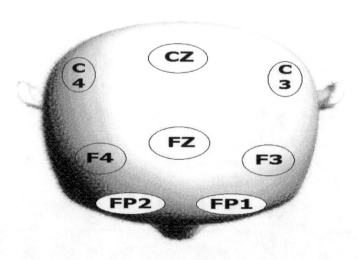

DATE

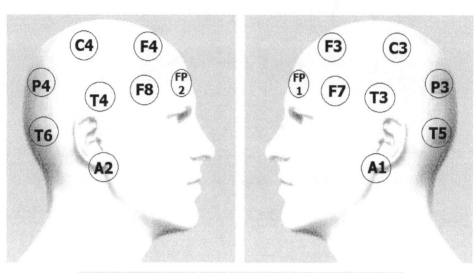

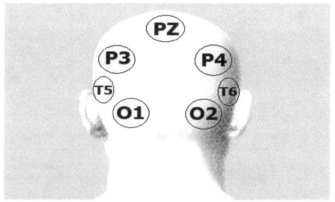

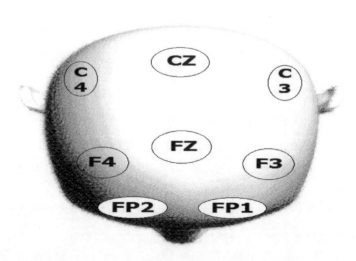

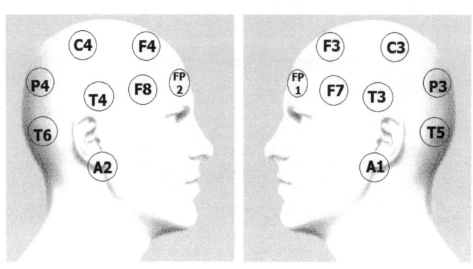

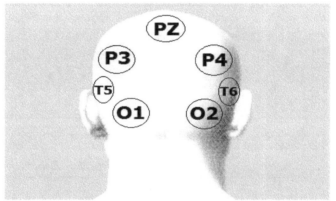

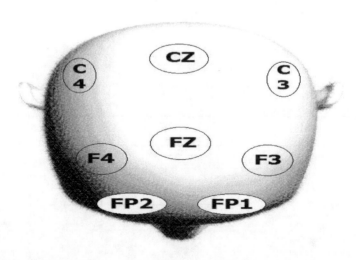

DATE

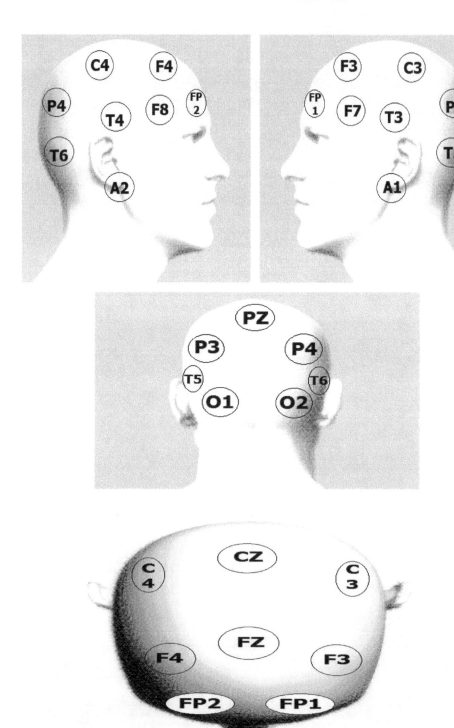

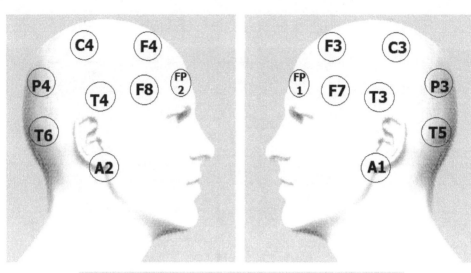

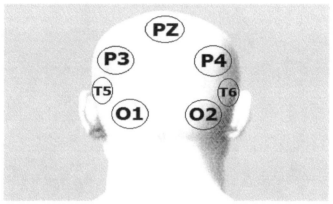

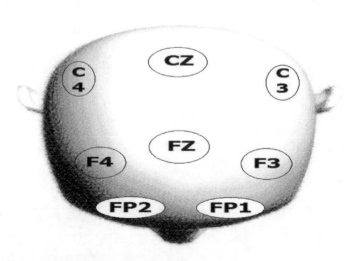

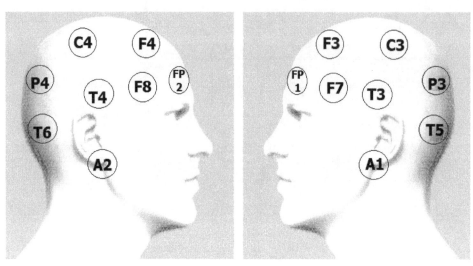

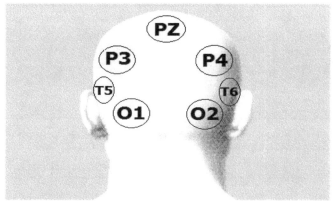

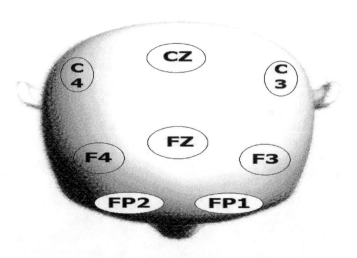

DATE

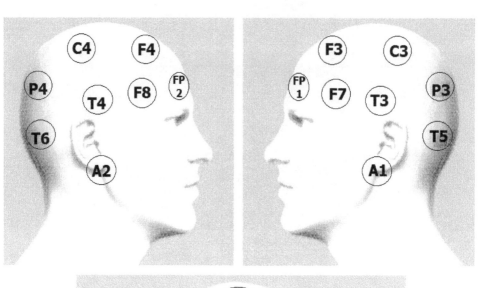

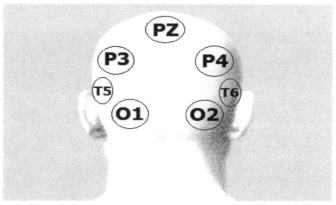

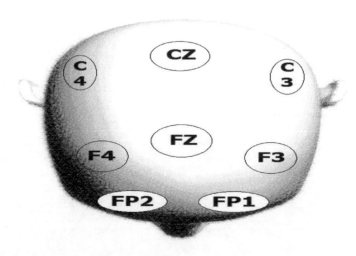

DATE

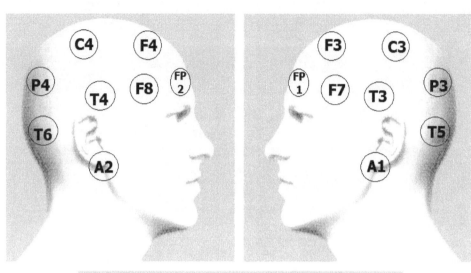

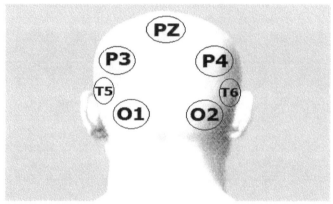

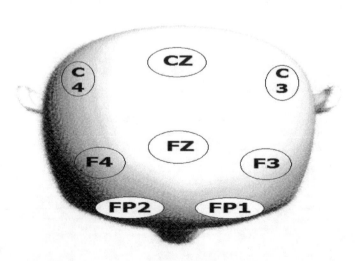

DATE

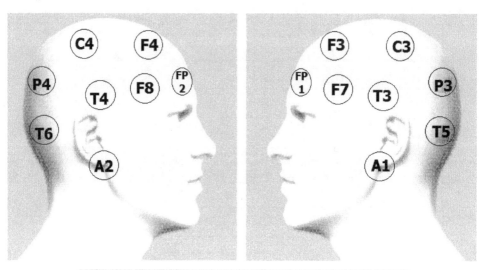

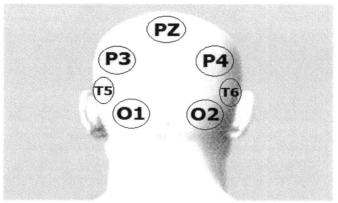

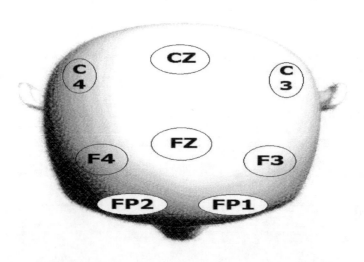

DATE

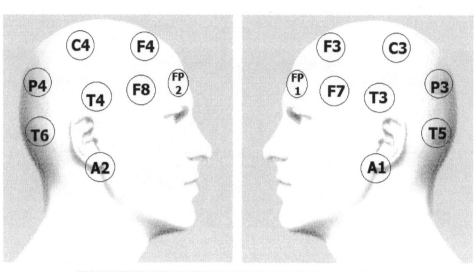

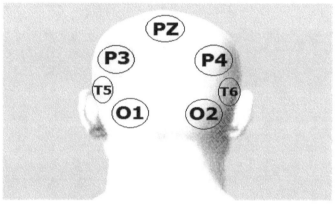

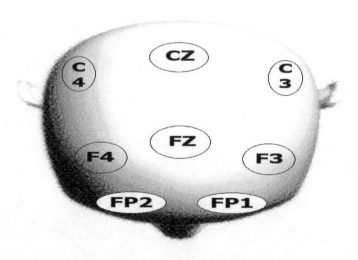

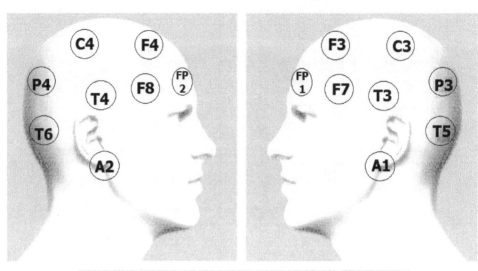

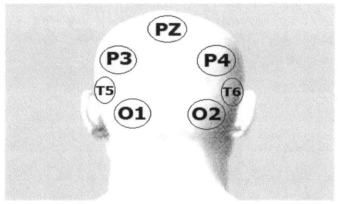

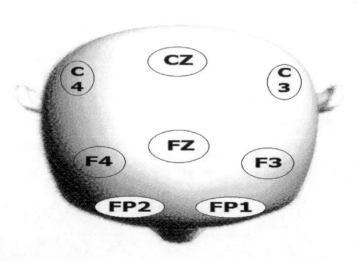

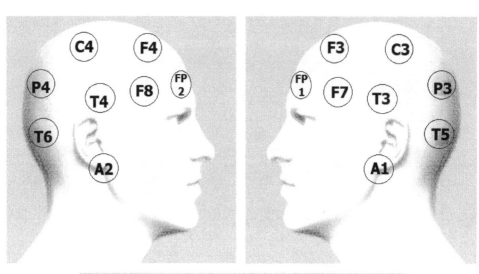

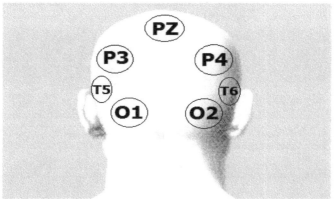

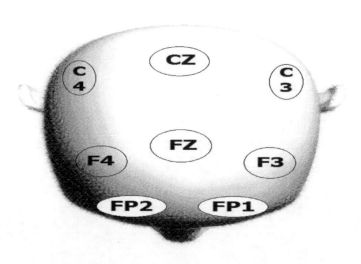

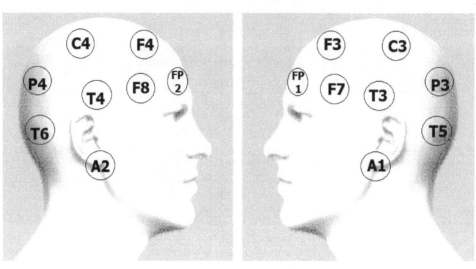

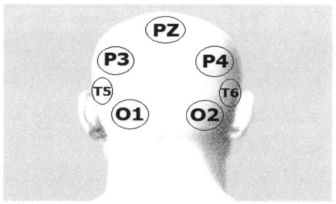

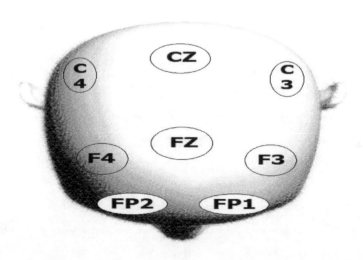

DATE

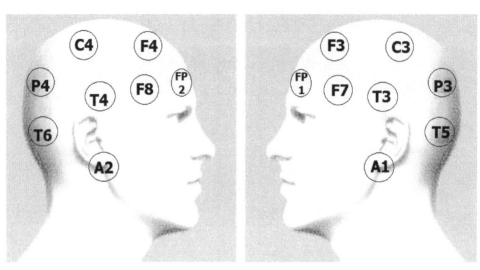

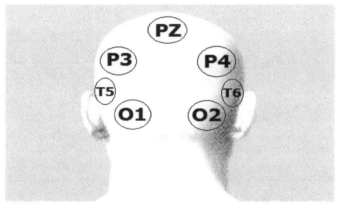

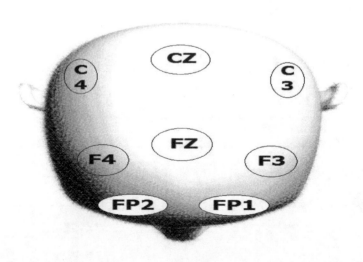

DATE

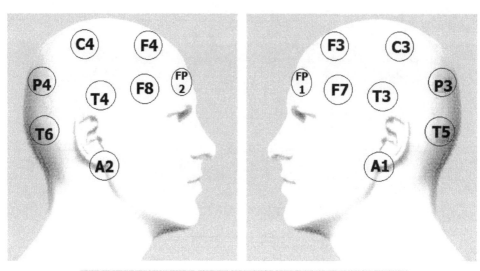

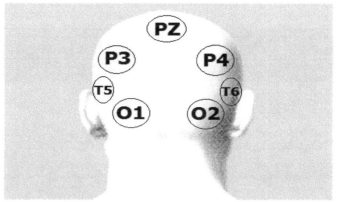

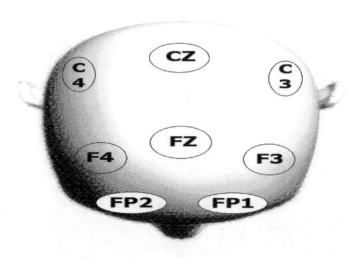

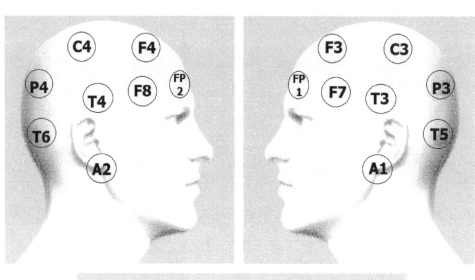

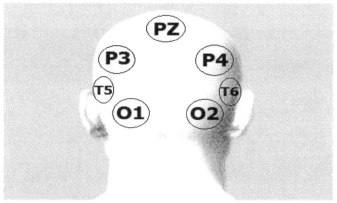

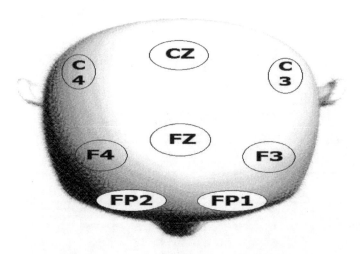

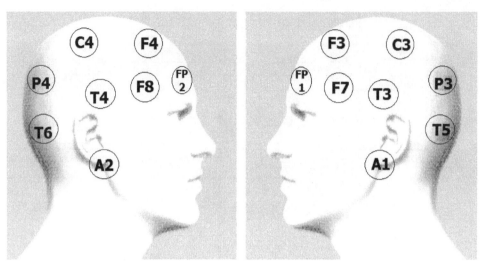

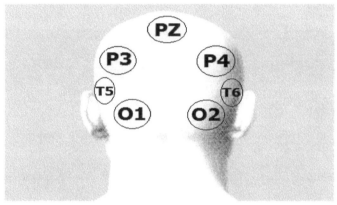

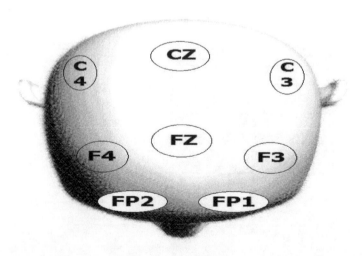

DATE

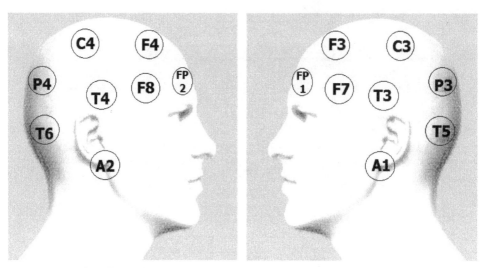

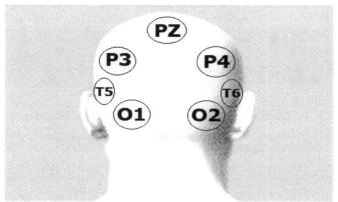

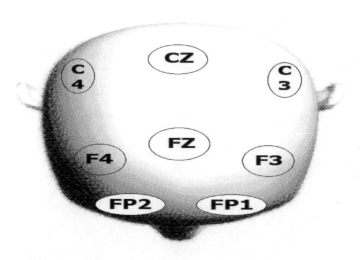

DATE

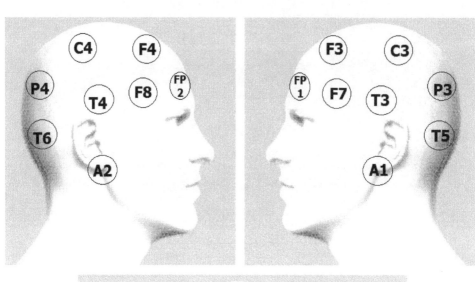

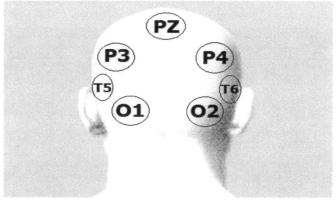

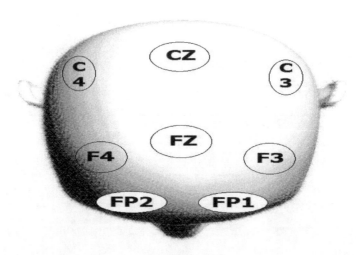

DATE

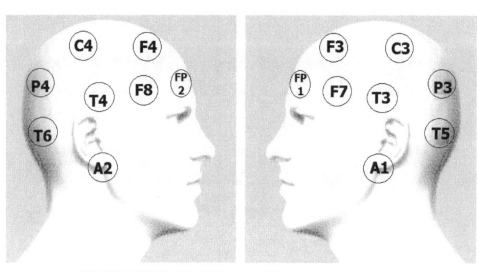

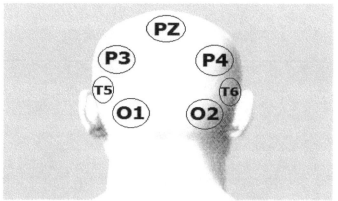

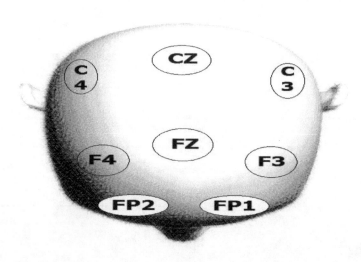

DATE

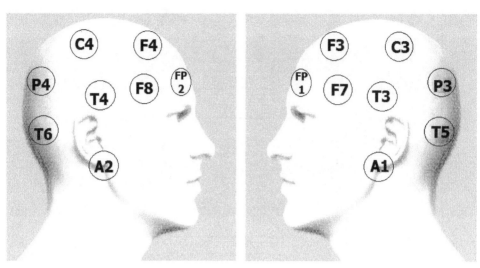

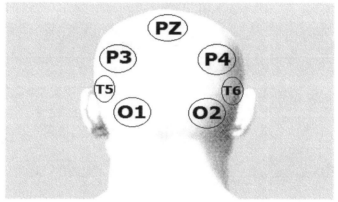

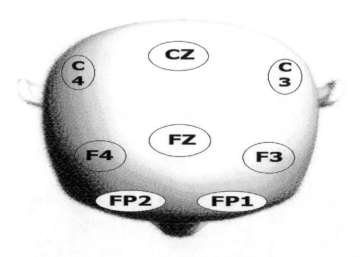

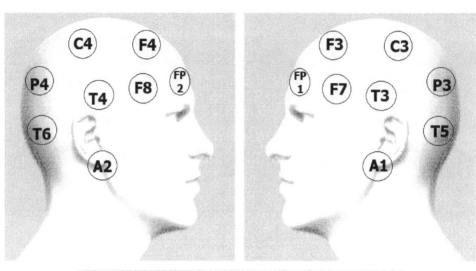

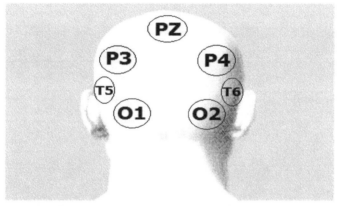

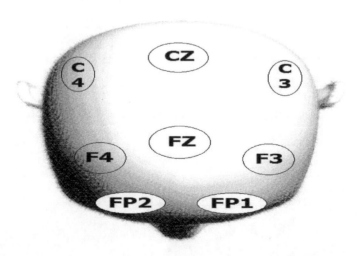

DATE

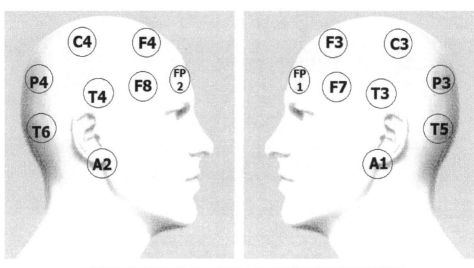

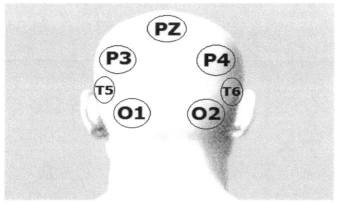

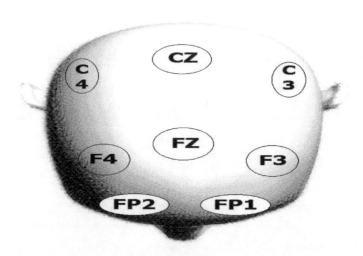

DATE

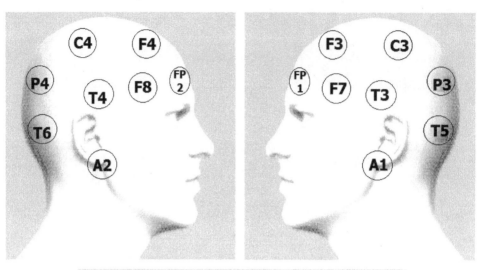

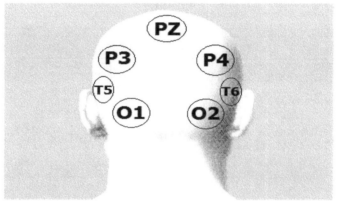

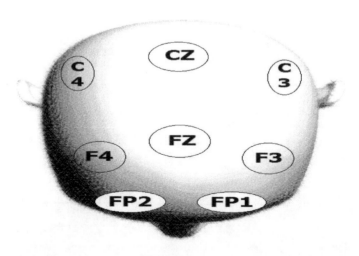

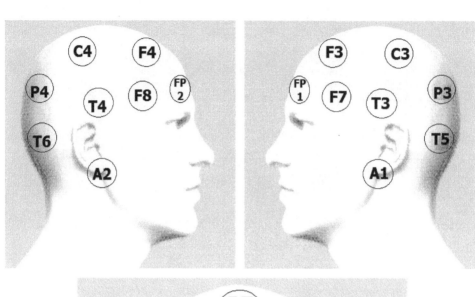

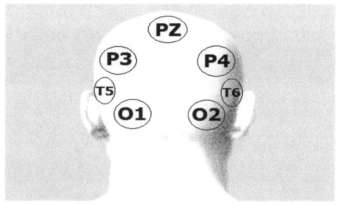

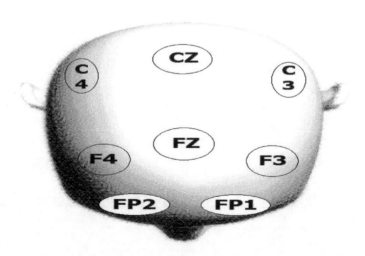

DATE

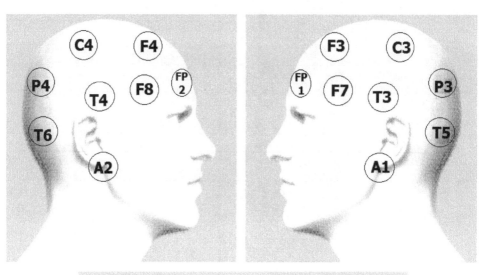

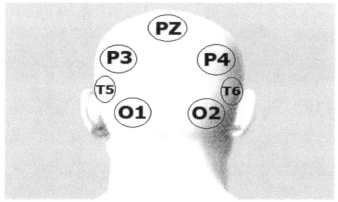

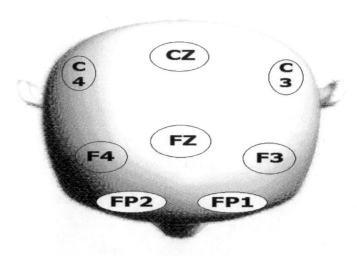

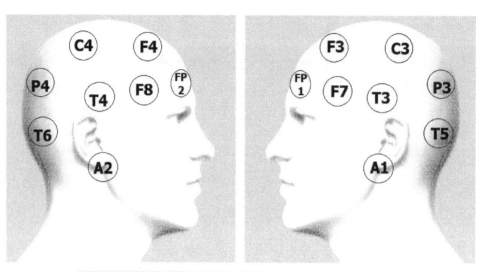

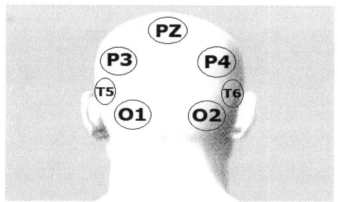

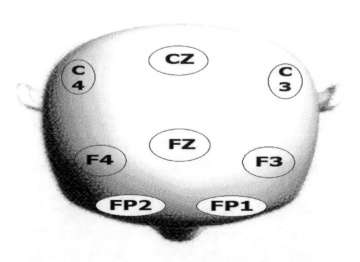

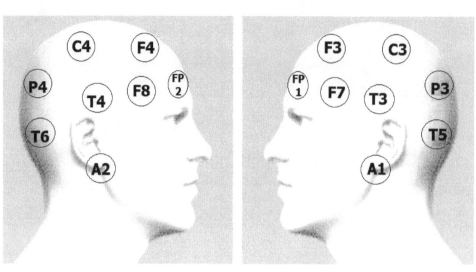

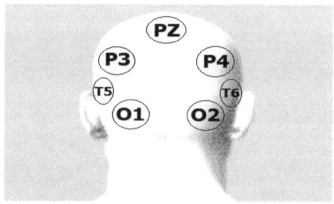

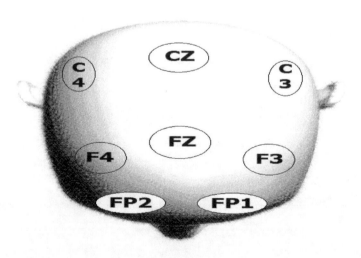

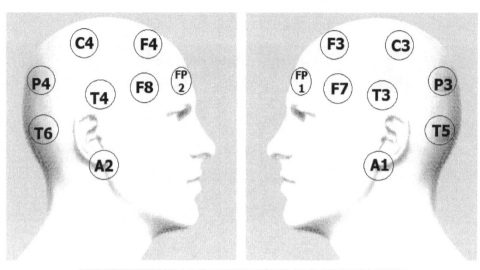

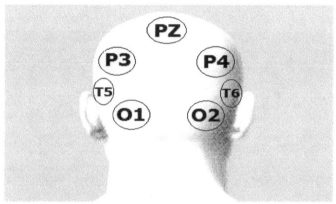

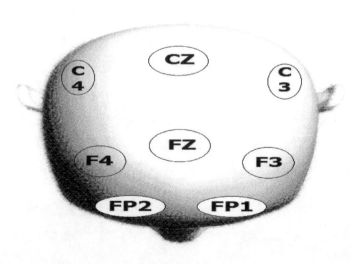

DATE

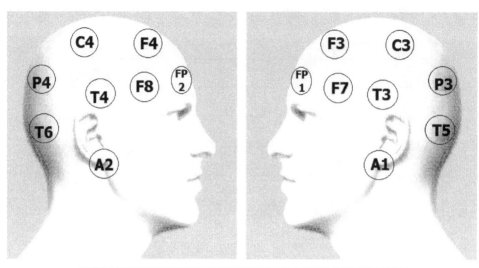

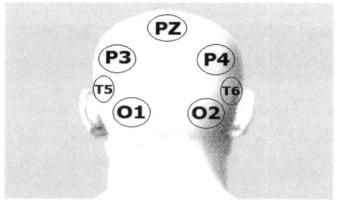

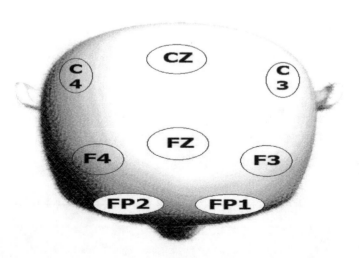

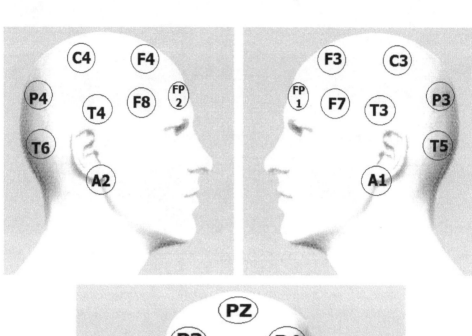

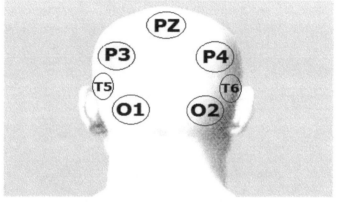

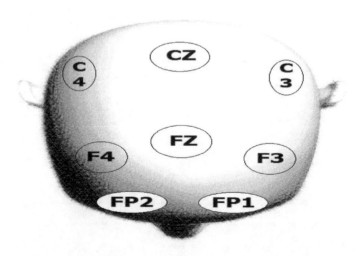

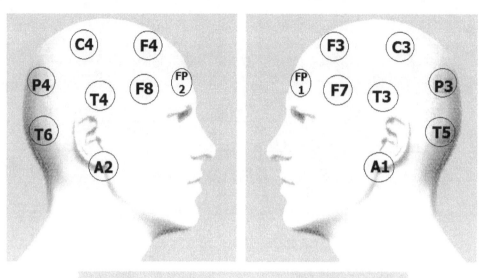

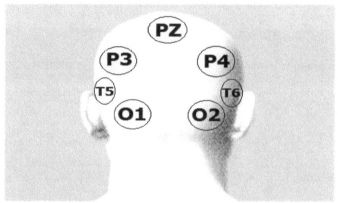

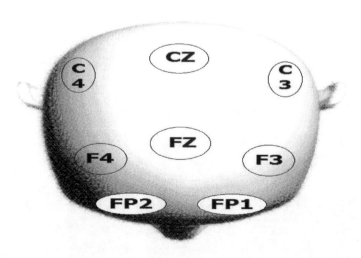

DATE

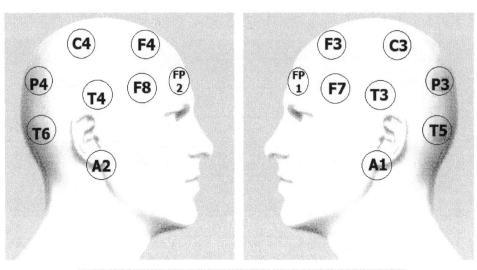

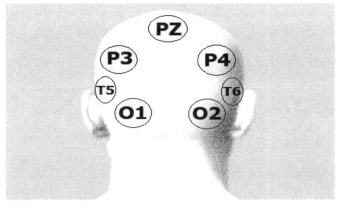

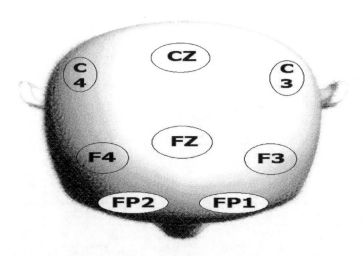

DATE

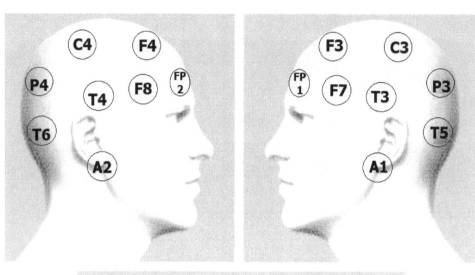

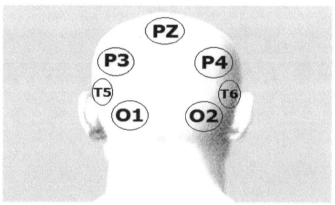

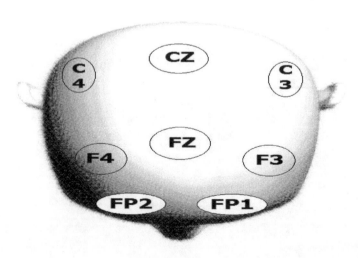

DATE

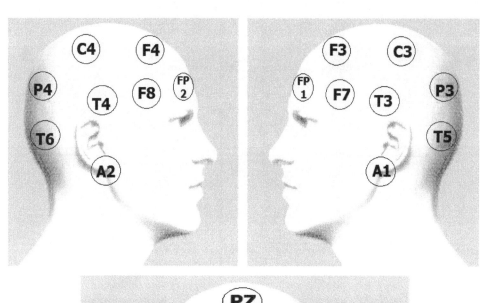

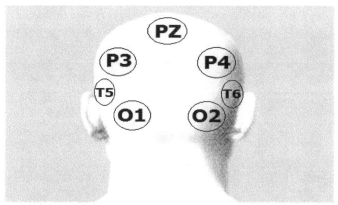

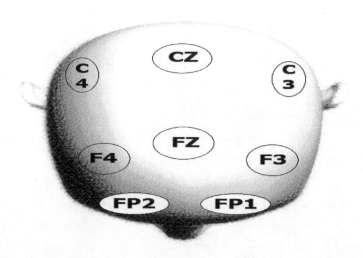

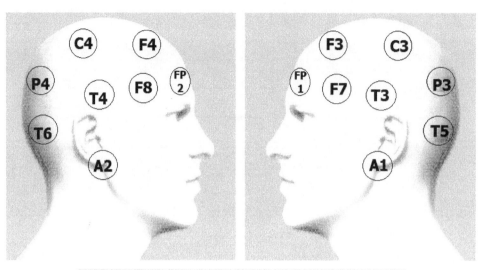

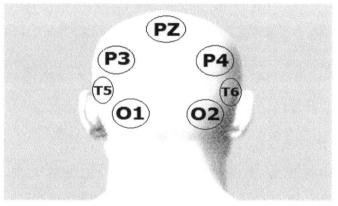

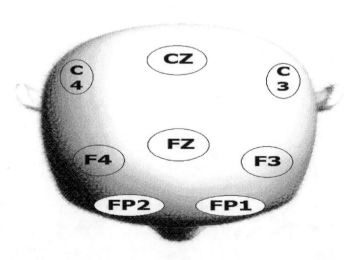

DATE

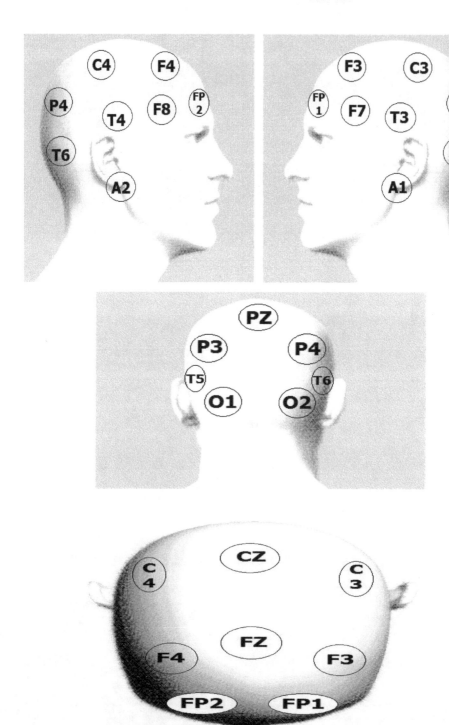

DATE

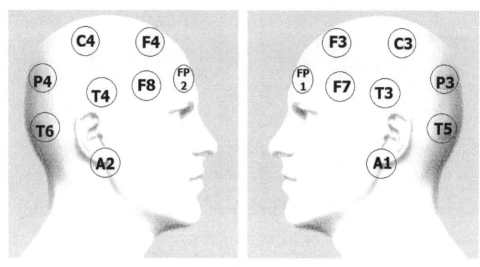

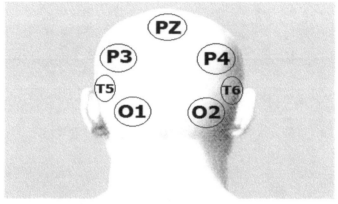

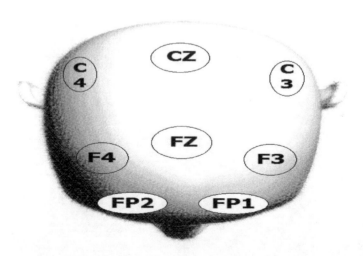

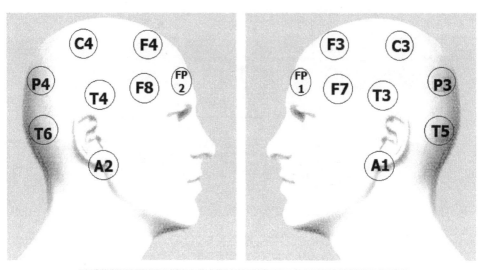

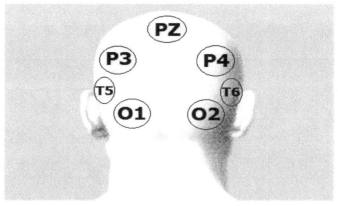

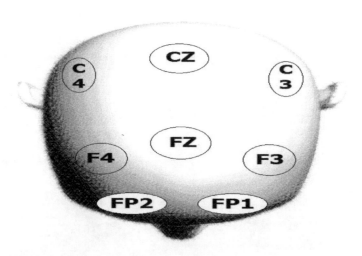

DATE

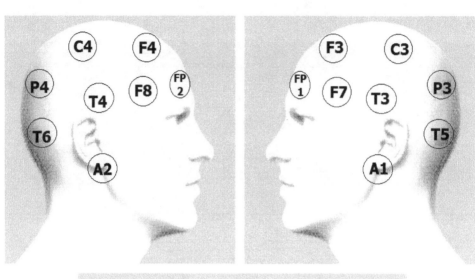

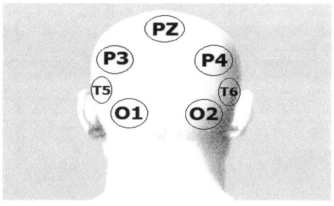

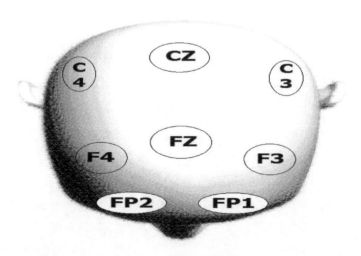